The Bee

Friend of the Flowers

Text and Photographs
by Paul Starosta

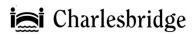 Charlesbridge

Photographs copyright © 1991 by Paul Starosta
Copyright © 1991 by Éditions Milan
Original edition first published by Éditions Milan under the title *l' abeille, amie des fleurs*.
300 rue Léon-Joulin, 31101 Toulouse Cedex 100, France

Copyright © 1992 by Charlesbridge Publishing
Library of Congress Catalog Card Number 92-74503
ISBN: 0-88106-430-0
Published by Charlesbridge Publishing, 85 Main Street, Watertown, MA 02472 • (617) 926-0329
www.charlesbridge.com
Printed in Korea
10 9 8 7 6 5 4

Little bees quickly learn which flowers are full of nectar. This bee will visit about two hundred flowers before it returns to the hive.

Into the flowers

It is springtime, when the warmth of the sun awakens all of nature. The air is mild and carries the scent of the first flowers.

A crowd of buzzing insects starts out for the day. A little honey bee is eager to go, too. But first, she flutters slowly around the hive to get her bearings. Then, sure of finding her way home, she zips off at almost ten miles an hour.

Amidst all the colors and scents, she chooses the flowers that offer the most nectar.

Unable to see red, the bee uses ultraviolet light to see colors that people can see only with a special kind of photograph.

This is how the field of flowers looks to a bee.

The honeybee's basket

The honeybee uses her straw-like tongue to suck up a sweet liquid, called nectar, from each flower. She stores the nectar in a special, small stomach called a honey sack.

As the bee walks on the flower and wiggles around, she shakes it and ends up covered in a golden dust. The dust is made up of tiny grains of pollen. The bee uses little brushes on her front legs to clean herself. She rolls the pollen into little balls and puts it into pollen baskets on her back legs.

Once she has loaded the baskets and drunk her fill of nectar, the bee flies around the area to make sure she will remember the place. Then, weighted down, she returns home.

Danger lurks in many places. This bee did not see the spider hiding on the flower.

Stick out your tongue! Don't worry about the pollen that falls on your back! These are the lessons each bee must learn in order to gather nectar and pollen.

Nothing beats a dandelion for filling those baskets with golden pollen.

When it is time to return to the hive, the bee finds her way in relation to the sun. With two compound eyes, she can tell where the sun is, even when clouds cover it.

This box is home to a hive of about 40,000 bees.

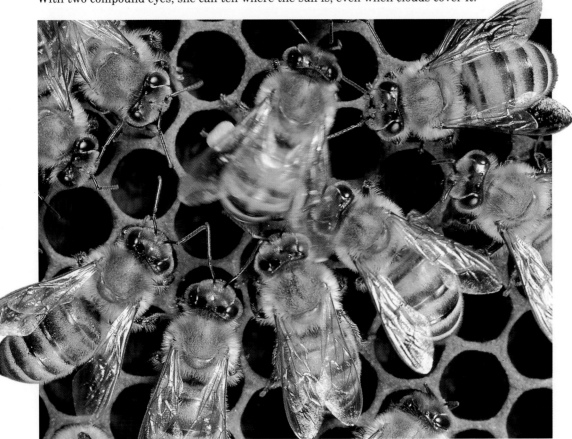

The little bee communicates with others from her hive by dancing.

Have a taste of this nectar. I'll tell you where to find more of it. (Sharing is natural for bees.)

Bees trying to enter the hive have to pass the guardians. Only members are allowed!

The dance of the bee

When the hive is in sight, the bee hurries to share her harvest. At the entrance, the guardians stop her to check whether or not she belongs to the hive. They finally agree that she does, and allow her to go in.

Inside, in the dark, thousands of bees rustle their wings. She touches one and offers a bit of the nectar she has brought home. Then, after a few other exchanges, she begins a dance that shows the others the way to the flowers. The shorter the distance to the flowers, the faster she dances. Following her directions, the other bees fly off, sure of a good harvest.

Making honey

Meanwhile, the bees in the hive pass the nectar from one honey sack to another. With each exchange, the nectar is changed a little bit until it becomes honey. The honey is placed in one of the little six-sided cells in the honeycomb. As fast as the workers can bring new nectar, the bees in the hive make and fill new honeycombs.

One last job is left. The honey is still too watery. Time for the fanners to get to work! Hovering over the cells, they flap their wings to make cool air circulate. The hive cools down, and the honey thickens.

The bees adjust the temperature of the hive so well they are like living air conditioners. Amazing!

On this slice of honeycomb, you can see how pollen is packed into the cells. It is an important food for young bees.

A bee's tongue is as good as a straw for sucking the nectar out cf flowers or for putting it into the cells of the honeycomb.

These bees are unloading their baskets of pollen. Other bees will take care of packing the pollen into the cells.

Beating their wings for hours, the fanners cool and thicken the honey.

This bee makes wax and uses each little flake to make new six-sided cells.

Cells filled with honey are capped with wax so that moisture cannot get in.

The waxmakers always work in groups. To produce two pounds of wax, they must eat twenty pounds of honey.

Wax for building

Thanks to the fanners, the honey has become thick enough. Twelve to sixteen day old bees close up the cells with wax. Starting when they are 12 days old, bees are able to secrete wax from special glands on their stomachs. The waxmakers use the wax for building the cells of the hive.

In the hive, each bee has its job. Bees do different jobs as they get older and as the needs of the hive change. Each bee may be a sweeper, brooder, nurse, waxmaker, fanner, and guardian. There is one bee, just one out of all the thousands of bees in the hive, who has a special job for its whole life — the queen.

The queen bee

In the middle of a little circle of workers lives the mother of all the bees in the hive. The young workers feed, protect, and care for her. They are her servants. As the queen moves forward, the circle of servants follows.

The queen looks into an empty cell and, satisfied that it is clean, turns around and lays an egg in it. She lays eggs all day. There is no time to lose. She takes advantage of the warm season to lay about 1,500 eggs each day.

Fortunately, this is her only job. Taking care of this huge family is the job of the brooders and the nurses.

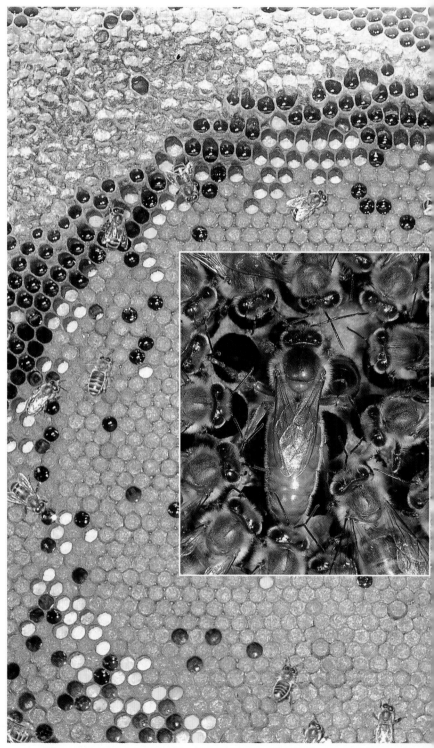

The queen is surrounded by her servants who feed and watch over her.

14

The queen lays eggs in the middle of the comb. The workers bring supplies of pollen and honey to the surrounding cells. The nurses will eat this food and use it to feed the larva that will hatch from the eggs.

Even though the queen lays the eggs straight up-and-down, gradually they tip over. During one year, the queen may lay as many as two hundred thousand eggs!

In summer, the queen lays only female eggs. They will hatch into larva in three days.

15

In six days, the larva have grown so much that they weigh five hundred times the weight of the egg. Now, they fill their cells.

No days off for the nurses. They have to feed each larva more than 10,000 times!

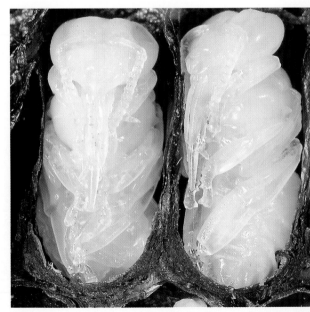

Each larva weaves a cocoon of silk. Then it changes and grows for 21 days when it will become a young bee.

Two menus for the larva

The brooders keep the cells at an even temperature (95°F) by fanning their wings. After three days, a little white larva hatches out of each egg. It looks like a tiny worm. The nurses then begin to feed royal jelly to the larva. This food is very high in protein, and can only be made by the nurses.

On the third day, the nurses change the menu to a mixture of water, pollen, and honey. After four days of this food, each cell is closed again with a wax seal. The larva weaves a cocoon and grows and changes.

Breaking the seal which kept it safe, a bee is born in the darkness of its hive. It will live for about 5 weeks, first doing jobs in the hive, later flying out to gather nectar and pollen.

The queen abandons her hive

When the hive is full and crowded, the bees know what to do. First, a group of workers enlarges the cells around a few eggs. As soon as they hatch, these privileged larva will be fed on a steady diet of royal jelly. Their menu will not change. This will make them grow into queen bees.

The old queen senses that there will be a new queen so she flies off. Workers and drones follow in a swarm of thousands of bees.

When they find an appropriate spot, the workers go out to gather nectar and pollen, and the waxmakers begin to build cells. As soon as the cells are ready, the queen lays eggs in them. It is the beginning of a whole new hive!

This swarm has stopped on a branch. They are looking for a hollow tree, or any other suitable place to start a new home. Scouts dance on the cluster to show which way to go.

18

These two compound eyes have seven thousand facets each. No doubt about it, these are the large eyes of a male, or drone, hatching.

As soon as a new home is chosen, the workers set out to collect nectar and pollen.

The drones of many hives gather in flight to mate with
the new queen.

The cell of a new queen is much larger than the other cells.

Long live the new queen

Meanwhile, back at the old hive, the colony is orphaned. The brooders and nurses will help a new queen to grow. In enlarged cells, the eggs hatch. These larva are fed royal jelly for seven days. Then, they are closed in their cells with wax seals.

After nine days, a new queen tears open her cell. She finds and kills the other queens before they can hatch. Then, the new queen joins the drones in flight. About ten of them mate with her and die right away. The other drones will die when winter comes.

After her one flight, the queen gives up blue skies forever for the kingdom of her dark hive. Her life then is devoted to laying eggs, and more eggs . . .

The queen, at birth, weighs more than twice as much as a worker. When the new queen emerges from her cell, she comes out the bottom.

Supplies for winter

During the winter, the bees must stay in the hive to keep warm. There are too many mouths to feed, so any drones are driven out. The workers use the last warm days to complete their store of supplies and to seal any cracks in the hive with wax.

The snow insulates the hive like a winter coat.

There may be twenty thousand bees huddling together to stay warm inside the hive. The bees can live up to five months during the winter resting period.

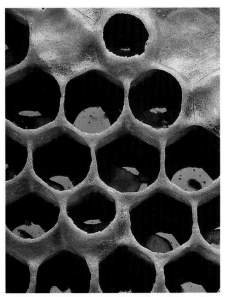

Even in winter, the bees must eat. With twenty-six pounds of honey in the honeycombs, they will have no problem surviving until spring.

It is wintertime, and it is too cold to go out. The queen has stopped laying eggs, so it is not necessary to keep the temperature in the hive at an even 95°F.

The bees gather around the center of the hive and their queen. They have everything they need to stay warm. As they eat up the honey stored in one part of the hive, they move gradually to another part. With springtime's first warmth, they will begin their very busy yearly cycle again.

Bee farming

Bees are farmed just like sheep or cows. Bees are raised by beekeepers. Honeybees and silk worms are the only insects that people farm. Bees are very important insects because they pollinate flowers so that fruits and vegetables will grow. In addition to the honey we take from the bees, we make lotions, candles, and other products from beeswax.

Handling bees

Beekeepers wear special gloves, and hats with veils that hang down around their faces. They pump smoke into the hive. When the bees smell smoke, they are less likely to sting. The beekeepers open the hive and take out a frame full of honeycomb. They do not disturb the queen and her eggs which are hatching in the bottom of the hive in a special place called a brood chamber.

Wonderful honey

Bees store more honey than they need as food during the winter. The beekeeper can take seven or eight pounds without harming the bees. The beekeeper may also take the comb itself for its wax, or for the pollen and royal jelly stored in it. Beekeepers do not need to kill their hives in order to enjoy a good harvest.

Kinds of bees

There are many breeds of bees: Italian, Caucasian, Tellian, and Cypriot are a few. Some breeds are better in colder climates, some are gentler, others are more productive. The so-called 'killer bee' is really just an African bee that was brought to South America because it can produce a lot of honey. Unfortunately, these bees sometimes attack people or animals that get too close to their hives.

Pollination

Each time a bee visits a flower, pollen rubs onto its body. In the next flower, it bumps into the stigma and deposits grains of pollen. This is how flowers are fertilized. It is called pollination.

Stings

When the bee stings another insect, the stinger comes out without any problem. But in our elastic skin, it is held in by the little bumps at its tip. If a bee stings a person, it will leave the stinger and part of its body hooked to the person's skin. The bee will die. Bees only attack to defend their hive, not while gathering honey. We can watch them without risk on flowers, but it is a good idea not to go near a hive.

If people try to remove the stinger by grabbing hold of it with their thumb and index finger, they will squeeze more venom into themselves from the sack attached to the stinger.

The bee family

Like all insects, bees have six legs. They belong to the species *apis*. Members of this family gather nectar and pollen to feed their larva. Some bees live alone, but honeybees must live in a colony that is part of a hive.

Bumblebees
Bumblebees are big, square-shaped bees. They live in little colonies of a few hundred bumblebees. In the Fall, the queen, the drones, and the workers die. Only a few fertilized females will live through the winter to begin a new underground nest the following spring.

The carpenter bee lives alone. The female digs a hole in dead wood. It places some nectar and pollen in the bottom of this nest and lays an egg. After sealing the nest with a mixture of sawdust and saliva, she starts the same operation over. At the end of her work, she has a column of seven or eight cells, each containing a larva and its food.

▼

◄ It is yellow and black, but no doubt about it, this is a wasp. These cousins of the bees build paper nests. They feed other insects to their larva. In wintertime, the colony disappears, except for a few fertilized females who, in the spring, will each become the queen of a new wasp nest. A wasp's stinger is smooth at the tip so it easily comes out of a person's skin. One wasp can sting many times.